100 SMALL WAYS TO

QUIT
WORRYING

100 SMALL WAYS TO
QUIT
WORRYING

NB

NEW BURLINGTON

A QUARTO BOOK

First published in the UK in 2017 by
New Burlington Press
The Old Brewery
6 Blundell Street
London N7 9BH

QUAR.MSWQW

ISBN: 978-0-85762-181-8

10 9 8 7 6 5 4 3 2 1

Conceived, designed,and produced by
Quarto Publishing plc
The Old Brewery
6 Blundell Street
London N7 9BH

Project editor: Kate Burkett
Senior designer: Martina Calvio
Proofreader: Caroline West
Illustrator: Rosie Scott
Art director: Caroline Guest
Creative director: Moira Clinch
Publisher: Samantha Warrington

Printed in China by 1010 Printing
International Ltd.

MIX
Paper from
responsible sources
FSC® C016973
www.fsc.org

FOREWORD

I believe that worry is the greatest threat to realising your potential. No matter what you choose to do in your life, nothing will endeavour to stop you in your tracks like this treacherous foe, the only imaginary enemy blocking the gates that lead to your dreams.

Worry is a wish for what you don't want, so if you already have plenty of what you don't want, choose your weapon from the 100 listed herein and bolt the door when worry wriggles its way into your weekend, armed with a malicious intention to wreck everything you have worked so hard for. Who would you be if you didn't worry? What would you do if your wishes came true? Remember this: As long as you are filled with worry, there is no room in your life for magic, miracles, happiness – and love.

Oliver Luke Delorie

MAKE A NEW FRIEND

What did you do the first day of school?
Probably played with some new kids. What
did you do the first day of your new job?
Probably met some new colleagues and
coworkers. What did you do at the family
reunion? Probably met some long-lost
relatives. Unless you like living under a
rock, getting a glimpse into a new way of
living is the spice of life. What do you
love to do? There are others just like you
out there looking for activity partners,
business partners and play partners. Put
yourself out there and stop worrying that
you will always be alone.

Friends help you cope with
the ups and downs of life.

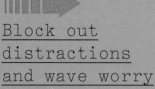

2

CLOSE YOUR EYES

Are you feeling overwhelmed? What if you could focus on one thing at a time? Would you worry less? When you are bombarded with visual stimulation, close your eyes and open your mind. Block out the world and let the movie in your imagination play. If your comedy suddenly turns to tragedy and you start worrying, open your eyes, take another deep breath and with something positive in mind, consciously squash any feelings of anxiety by giving your eyes (and your worries) another rest.

Block out distractions and wave worry goodbye.

3

SET AN EXAMPLE

Are you surrounded by kids, nieces, nephews, family friends, students, young athletes, artists or entrepreneurs that look up to you? If the answer is yes, unless you are biting your nails and trembling with fear in front of them, you are trust personified. Simply knowing more about a subject than someone else makes you an expert, and with power comes responsibility, so what are you worried about? When the people around you see how little you worry (or how best you hide it) you will inspire their trust, which is one of the best qualities you can model to others.

Set an example as a stoic soldier in the war against worry.

4 ⬤ LISTEN

You have two ears and one mouth. How about listening twice as much as you talk? My aunt gave me a bookmark when I was a child emblazoned with 'Listening is love in action' written in calligraphy. When you listen, you naturally stop thinking about yourself (and therefore worrying about your problems). Listening may also help you empathise with whomever you are listening to, which will also deepen your relationship (another way to reduce worry).

Are you listening or just waiting for your turn to speak?

'LISTENING is LOVE in Action'

5

FIND A ROLE MODEL

While a mentor is someone you may seek direct advice and guidance from, a role model arrangement is less structured. Your role model doesn't even have to know they are your role model. Who do you admire? Who do you envy, read about, or follow? What about this person inspires you? Tony Robbins, one of the most popular life coaches on the planet, believes in 'modelling' which means you basically copy how you think this person thinks, feels, and acts. What have you got to lose?

Who is living your dream life?
How do they think?
How do they act? Model them.

6

HAKUNA MATATA

A combination of *hakuna* (there is not here) and *matata* (plural form of problem), *hakuna matata* is Swahili for 'no worries'. According to Timon and Pumbaa of *The Lion King*, these two words will solve all your problems. And if you have any doubts, maybe it's time to watch (or re-visit) one of Disney's classic films. Yes, adopting such a breezy, carefree attitude in times of trouble can seem aloof to those who like to sweat the small stuff, though remember there are many ways to look at any situation.

Australians coined 'No Worries' as their national motto in 1978.

7

ASK FOR FORGIVENESS

If you are human, you have done or said (or not done or have left unsaid) something you would like to absolve yourself of. Al Pacino said in *The Devil's Advocate*: 'Guilt is like a bag of bricks. All you have to do is put it down.' So why suffer any more? If you have unintentionally caused harm or hurt the ones you love (who hasn't?) and dwell on said transgressions and worry yourself to sleep every night, it's time to take the high road, swallow your pride and pick up the phone.

<u>Weak people cannot forgive. Forgiveness is the custom of the strong.</u>

TAKE A DEEP BREATH

Charlie Brown said, 'I've developed a new philosophy. I only dread one day at a time.' People tend to worry because they are either thinking about the future or reliving the past. The solution to this dual dilemma is deep diaphragmatic breathing. Breathe in slowly through your nose, hold it for five seconds, then let it out slowly through your mouth. Do it again, because your brain and body need oxygen as much as they need water. Deep breathing will always calm you down, no matter what you are worrying about.

The more calm you are, the less you worry.

9 GET A GUARD DOG

Not just a best friend, a canine replete with canines will deter most intruders and wrong-doers and provide another layer of protection around you, your loved ones and your personal possessions. Both companion and comrade, your pooch is ready to take up arms at the first sign of danger. So, as long as you love and care for him/her, your little assassin will serve you all of his/her days. Even a tame, gentle breed will intimidate the enemy (if not fight tooth-and-nail to defend you).

Be careful when it comes to naming your furry friend, because 'Fluffy, attack!' may not strike fear into the hearts of ne'er-do-wells.

 # 10 GET MORE SLEEP

How do you feel when you don't get enough sleep? After a sleepless night, our memories, weight and overall health are affected. And not in a good way. According to the Center for Disease Control, sleeping issues are a public health epidemic. If you get more sleep, your brain and body will function better. And if your brain and body function better, you will worry less. And when you worry less, you will be happier. And you may have better sex, build muscle, learn quicker and stay fit. Geez, where do I sign?

It's past
your bedtime.

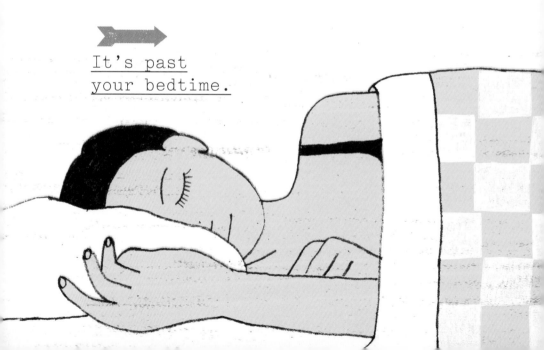

11

ACCEPT THINGS AS THEY ARE

Everything is as it should be. Could you change it even if you wanted to? Probably not, so let it be. Worry arises out of wanting things to be different than they are (as opposed to expecting things to be different). More stress, anxiety and worry come from not accepting things as they are than anything else. As hard as it seems, accepting things as they are is the way to happiness / enlightenment / contentment / satisfaction (if that is what you are after).

Most worry, stress and unhappiness arise from wishing things were different.

12 FACE A FEAR

What did you do the last time you faced a fear? You told yourself there was nothing to get so worked up about, didn't you? If you are reading this, you got through it (whatever it was). Still, you probably lose sleep wondering how a doctor's appointment, an overseas trip, a job interview or a presentation at work will turn out. But you know better! What is worse: Trembling under the covers at the sheer terror of imagined monsters lurking under the bed or taking a deep breath, flicking on the flashlight and expelling the evil spirits back to the invisible nothingness from whence they came?

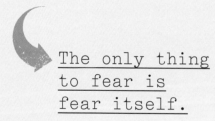

The only thing
to fear is
fear itself.

The monster under the bed is just as scared as you are, which is why he/she is hiding under the bed in the first place, and not jumping up and down yelling BOO! Call his her bluff by taking a peek under your bed. Do it now.

Imagine everyone naked when you are walking on stage to give a speech or presentation. There must be something to this, otherwise why would it be so popular a ploy to calm your nerves and put a smile on your face? Your audience wants you to succeed.

Going to the dentist doesn't have to be scary. If you are like most people, you are long overdue a check-up, but dentists offer full sedation (whatever that means) and, for those who like their funny bone tickled, laughing gas is a hoot!

Before your job interview do your due diligence on the company and on the personnel who will be interviewing you, and recruit a friend or loved one to grill you. The more prepared you are, the more professional you will appear. Believe you will get the job and act accordingly. It can't hurt.

If you fear flying you will be happy to know that, statistically, flying is the safest mode of travel. Avoid getting drunk to calm your nerves; there are natural and pharmaceutical remedies to ease your anxieties. If you want to get somewhere fast, flying is the way to go.

13

WALK IN NATURE

Spending any time outdoors will make you feel good. Nature is simple. And the simpler your life, the less you will worry. Walking is easy for most people, but you could hike, ride, climb, ski, board, float or fly your way through the world. Fresh air alone is often enough to boost your mood. Got your tickets for the next time the weather goes wild? And if you like your outdoors a little more tame, stroll through a city park in spring and marvel at the cherry blossoms.

The world is a garden planted just for you.

14

TURN OFF YOUR COMPUTER

There is an OFF button for a reason. Depending on how old (or young) you are, you may remember when computers were nothing more than super-sized calculators designed to perform simple mathematical calculations on autopilot. Going on a technology fast will ease your mind (and thus subdue your worries that you aren't keeping up appearances on your favourite social media sites).

Unplug for a day. Or a week. Go on a technology fast. Remember the good old days?

SLOW DOWN

When you are worried about something, your thoughts, feelings and/or actions are breaking the speed limit. And speed kills. So take it easy. What's the rush? The slower you drive, the less fuel you consume, the safer everyone is and the more pleasant your drive. On a personal level, the same philosophy applies, so take it easy and take the time to smell the roses.

 Those that run fast stumble.

16

BUY SOME INSURANCE

The more insurance you have, the less
you will worry. Yet insurance salespeople
(and the policies they sell) are the
least popular 'products' on the planet.
You are basically betting on bad stuff
happening. Some people say the odds are
stacked against you, especially the older
you get. But it's up to you. The money
you spend on monthly premiums could just
as easily be spent on experiences-of-a-
lifetime that are worth every penny.

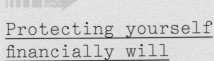

Protecting yourself
financially will
ease your mind.

LEARN TO KNIT

Grandmothers knit for a reason. Calming and productive, knitting is a time-honoured craft. Functional (and often beautiful), looping and knotting the spun wool of those cuddly creatures known as sheep can calm even the most tense of nervous systems. In knitter's lingo, the entire process can be summed up in three simple steps: cast-on, knit a row, cast-off. Not only is knitting therapeutic, but you also get to act like a kitten and play with a ball of wool. Woohoo!

<u>Nothing can go terribly wrong when you are knitting.</u>

18

EAT A SALAD

Ever since you were a kid you have heard that you are what you eat. Are you a cheeseburger? A plate of mussels and frites? A pan of paella? Ever wanted to 'be' a salad? With salad, there are no rules. Add some smoked fish or cheese or tofu. Whip up any type of dressing you like (nearly any flavour is available from your local supermarket). And if you are feeling adventurous, kick it up a notch with some shredded kale, broccoli or cabbage for your daily dose of cruciferous roughage, and if you want to keep the doctor away, slice up an apple and add it to the mix.

Salad is an art form.

LEARN SELF DEFENCE

If you are seriously concerned for your personal safety whenever you are out after dark (or even during the day), a proven way to mute the heebie-jeebies is to take a self-defence course. Man or woman, old or young, feeling physically safe in the world is mission-critical. Put your worries to bed so you can have some fun.

High-ya!

20 DELEGATE

Not only is entrusting others with responsibility the secret of good time management (and thus increased productivity, LESS STRESS and ultimately more personal and professional success), but also makes your life easier. The more effectively you delegate, the more you can RELAX once in a while. Delegating is crucial if you manage children, coworkers, friends or volunteers. Learn THIS SKILL and watch the weight evaporate from your shoulders.

There is an old saying that goes something like this:

'For general peace of mind, resign as general manager of the universe.'

To this I would add:

'By delegating.'

 You don't have to do everything yourself!

FORGIVE SOMEONE

This is a big one. No matter what you believe, or who you listen to, or what you were taught, many people mention forgiveness as the answer to every conflict, problem, struggle and worry in their lives. Simple as it sounds, it can be the hardest act to follow. Especially when we feel we have been harmed beyond redemption. Is hate not poison? Chances are, the people who have slighted us don't even recall what happened. So why carry around so much distrust, anger, rage and shame when we could simply acknowledge our feelings and choose to be kind, instead of right?

'Forgive them father, for they know not what they do.' ~ Jesus

22

BE GRATEFUL

Hawaiian shamans believe the two most
powerful words in the English language are
'Thank You'. Not that Hawaiian shamans
have discovered all the keys to happiness,
success and a worry-free existence, though
every wise person in existence has alluded
to the emotional freedom available to
those who are grateful for every good (and
bad) thing in their life. Yes, it may be
difficult to accept things as they are, but
thousands of philosophers can't be wrong.
What bad could come from expressing a
little gratitude now and then, if not
every day?

Appreciation will dissolve
nearly every worry.

23

WRITE A LETTER TO YOUR FUTURE SELF

What are you proud of? What do you hold sacred? Who or what is important to you? Do you ever wonder what you will be like 20, 30, 40, 50 or 60 years from now? Why not write a letter to your future self (and hide it away for safe-keeping) describing your life, ambitions, passions, motivations, relationships and outlook on life as it is now?

Vent to your future self. What you worry about now will one day seem insignificant.

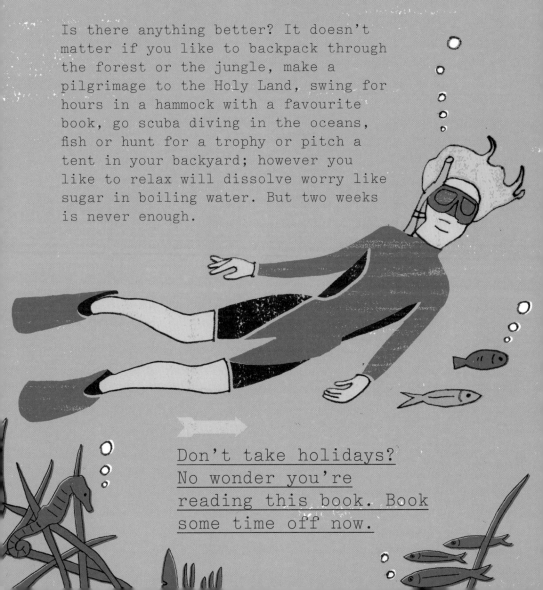

PLAN A HOLIDAY

Is there anything better? It doesn't matter if you like to backpack through the forest or the jungle, make a pilgrimage to the Holy Land, swing for hours in a hammock with a favourite book, go scuba diving in the oceans, fish or hunt for a trophy or pitch a tent in your backyard; however you like to relax will dissolve worry like sugar in boiling water. But two weeks is never enough.

Don't take holidays? No wonder you're reading this book. Book some time off now.

COUNT YOUR BLESSINGS

Can you walk? Talk? Do you have eyes? Ears? Arms and feet? Ten fingers? Ten toes? Friends or family? Food in the refrigerator? Clothes to keep you warm? Work? Options in life? It is easy to forget how much you have, especially when you are worried about (and thus focused on) what you don't. As you know, there are billions (thousands of millions) of people with much less. Worrying about this inequality will bog you down even more, so instead, count your blessings and consider how you may share the abundance you enjoy with others. In some cases, this is all that is required to cast worry aside.

Send a blessing and you will become one.

SPEND LESS TIME WITH WORRIERS

Just like some viruses are contagious, so is worry. Why would you want to expose yourself to bugs out to kill you? Gossip, tattling, back-stabbing, complaining and general negativity only serve to bring you down. Who needs more negativity in their life? The less time you spend with worriers, the less you will worry. So hang out with some motivated, positive thinkers instead. There is ample room in their club and they will always welcome you with open arms.

You are the average of the five people you spend the most time with.

27 ACCEPT CONSTRUCTIVE CRITICISM

Haters are gonna hate. Waiters are gonna wait. And potatoes are gonna potate! Seriously now, how you see yourself is often very different from how others see you (and perhaps how you really are). So ask for a (constructive) critique of you and your precious life, and heed the advice, provided it feels somewhat close-to-home. Tip: The more you deny something as absolutely-not-true, the more likely you could benefit from accepting it as part of what some counsellors refer to as your 'Achilles Heel'. Again, the more self-aware you become, the less you will worry.

No one's perfect (you may hear this often). But only take note of critique that rings true.

28 READ AN INSPIRING/ TRASHY BOOK

Expand your mind and use your imagination. You can't worry when you're distracted. Whether you prefer sensational romance or provocative self-help, books are dreams you hold in your hand. And when you're dreaming, you are probably not worrying. Many have gone before you and struggled, worried and stressed about everything (and more), so if you can read, you can instantly escape, calm or transcend your worries. The pen is truly mightier than the sword.

If you don't read a book, it can't help you.

29

CALL YOUR BEST FRIEND

Stevie Wonder sang, 'I just called to say I love you.' Everyone has a best friend. Even the geeks and nerds in high school had best friends (who were also unpopular). What are friends for? When you need them most, they are there. You would think nothing of fielding a call from your bestie at 3am if he or she really needed you, so if you are ever at the point of worry-beyond-worry, call your best friend. They are your BF for a reason.

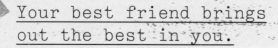

Your best friend brings out the best in you.

30

WALK THE DOG

Is your doggie all alone at home while
you are working hard to bring home the
dog food? All your mongrel wants is
to run around, sniff other doggies and
get some exercise. When you get home,
take the mutt around the neighbourhood
(not just around the block), because
the more interesting your pet's social
life, the less they will worry.

Get some fresh air. Exercise
washes worry away.

31

WATCH STAND UP COMEDY

Laughing reduces the stress hormone cortisol. This means that the more you laugh, the less you worry. There are thousands of hours of comedy available for free on various cable and subscription channels, as well as radio shows, podcasts and videos for you to chuckle at. All humour is not for everyone, though some wise crackers will have you rolling on the floor roaring with laughter and crying tears of joy.

Laughter is the best medicine.

32

WORK LESS

In a typical 8-hour shift (thanks to water-cooler conversation, personal emails, social media addiction and a preoccupation with concerns more pressing than work), most people only get four hours of work done. Is there any way you could manage to work less? Without work cramping your style and driving you to stress leave, what would life be like if you worked part-time instead? If you can simplify your life, working less for someone else will allow you to work more for yourself. Don't like it? Don't do it.

Work less and live more, so you can live more and worry less.

BUY HAND SANITISER

A microbe is a micro-organism that causes disease or fermentation (neither of which you want). If you can't wash your hands with soap and water, hand sanitiser will save the day. This stuff may not remove harmful chemicals such as pesticides from your hands and don't on any occasion swallow the stuff, no matter how much you think your internal flora and fauna may need cleansing. Instantly evaporating as you rub it into your hands, hand sanitiser will blunt any angst-due-to-worry concerns about cleanliness.

Not just for those with O.C.D., hand sanitiser is a quick fix for the worry warts (literally).

34

DRINK A GLASS OF WATER

Most people carry around a bottle of water nowadays. For good reason. Your body is made up of about 60% water, so you need regular replenishment to keep everything working in optimum balance. The experts say by the time you're thirsty, you are already dehydrated. Coffee, alcohol and fruit juice (although containing water) are no substitute for the real thing. How about clearer skin, more energy, less fatigue and fewer worries? If you answered yes, water is your fountain of youth.

Water will ease the pain of headaches due to worry.

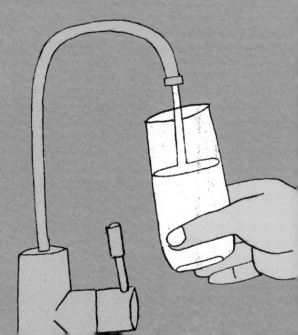

35

BUY A LOTTERY TICKET

Like getting drunk, this is a temporary
distraction from worry. If you are obsessed
with winning the lottery and dissolving
all your worries with money, you may want
to do some research before getting too
excited. If you are unhappy now, odds
are that nothing will change following a
financial windfall. Some believe the more
you have, the more you have to lose. As
such, the stress associated with winning
a fortune is often too much for people to
handle. But for a quick fix, gambling on an
inexpensive lottery ticket can be a fun way
to ease your worries. Just keep it all in
perspective, okay?

Bet on yourself instead.

MAKE A TO DO LIST

Your To-Do List is personal, so you can be as obsessive or as laid-back as you wish (no one has to know). The point is to keep your ideas / thoughts / worries all in one place so you can get an objective overview of what you would like to accomplish in your day / week / month / year / life. Creating a To-Do List will only weed out your worries if you actually do what is necessary to cross off each bullet point as it gets dealt with. Finally, efficiency experts say making a list will keep you organised, productive and efficient. What do you think?

Stop talking and start doing.

37 BAKE SOME CHOCOLATE CHIP COOKIES

Get out the flour, baking soda, salt, butter, sugar, eggs, vanilla, chocolate chips, cookie sheet, mixing bowl, hand mixer, spatula and wooden spoon. Preheat the oven. Find a recipe for the precise measurements of each ingredient and get to work, because in 30 minutes you may just step into bliss as you bite into a warm chocolate chip cookie. Cancel the appointment with your psychiatrist, because baking beats the worries into batter that tastes better than any anti-anxiety medication.

Omit the raisins, currants, cranberries, nuts, oatmeal, coconut, flax and hemp seeds to experience the pure joy of a simply sinful chocolate chip cookie.

LEARN TO MEDITATE

Meditating regularly will give you a glimpse of the place where two equals one (the place where worries don't exist). Experiencing what yogis refer to as duality can bring about profound changes in not only your psychology, but also your physiology. Deep breathing, mantras, stretching and yoga are known to expand consciousness. But why would you want to expand your consciousness? Because self-awareness is the closest thing to understanding why you exist in the first place.

Inner peace. What else is there (apart from chocolate chip cookies)?

GIVE SOMEONE A HUG

Two hundred years ago, an eleven-year-old child was found living in the forest, physiologically and psychologically considered an idiot. Psychologists eventually concluded that the child had been deprived of human touch. Want to relieve stress? Give someone a hug. Touch signals safety and trust, and it has a powerful effect on our emotions. The more you are touched, the more you will feel loved.

<u>Four hugs a day for survival, eight for maintenance, and twelve for growth.</u>

40

BUY A NEW PAIR OF SHOES

The average woman owns 20 pairs of
shoes. Some own more, some less
(women are on to something). Maybe
happy feet do equal a happy life
(and fewer fashion worries). For
instance, high heels metaphorically
raise your status. And perhaps there
are scientific / genetic / evolutionary
reasons for foot fetishes. New shoes
make you feel like a million bucks.
It's a temporary fix, but hey, gurus
all say 'be here now'.

You can never have too many shoes.

MAKE A LIST OF TEN NOUNS YOU USED TO ENJOY

What person, place or thing is troubling you? The opposite of brainstorming solutions to your problems is making a list of the people, places and things you enjoy most about life. Shifting your focus from how to solve problems to reminiscing about what brought you joy and excitement in the past can be enough to inspire new thoughts, actions and feelings. Rekindle the romance of the life, love and happiness you once enjoyed and free yourself from the reins of worry.

This activity will rekindle the spirit of joy inside you. And chase worry away.

If you think, 'My friends in high school were the best friends I ever had' then it's time to reconnect with them (or identify why they were the best friends you ever had) and organise a reunion, or create opportunities to re-experience the pleasure (and pain) of your glory days (just remember how a responsible adult would act in case things get wild).

Maybe backpacking around Europe or America for a year when you were young was the best time of your life; you were free to explore your limits, morals and capabilities. Do you miss the sense of adventure? Do you miss the sense of freedom? Your liberal point-of-view? New ideas, change and spontaneity are addictive, so how can you reignite your passions in a productive and creative way?

What was your favourite toy as a child? What was so enchanting about it? What did you dream of? Who did you want to be? Some child psychologists believe in the benefits of play therapy. No matter what harm or wrong or disaster or stress you have experienced, remembering what brought you joy as a child (or young adult) can quickly remind you of what made you feel safe, loved, cherished or appreciated as you were growing up. When times are tough and you are worried for your safety or emotional well-being, make a list of people, places and things that brought you peace and serenity, and you will vanquish worry forever.

42 GET SOME SUNSHINE

Like smiling, laughing, drinking water, sleeping, hugs, fun, singing, listening to your favourite music and the innumerable other ways to stop worrying suggested in this book, without the sun, nothing would exist. Stop and contemplate the gravity of this concept for a moment. Without the sun, you couldn't see anything. No colours. No light. Everything would be cold and dark and scary. People can lose their minds from lack of sunshine, so if you tend to worry about your health and happiness, a little Vitamin D may do you some good, especially if you live in the Northern Hemisphere.

Sunshine reduces cholesterol, so you can worry less about what you eat. Bonus!

43 SMILE

Do you worry when you are happy?
Of course not. And for good reason.
When you are smiling or laughing
or expressing joy, your brain is
releasing happy hormones into your
body, broadcasting to every cell
that all is well. Studies have shown
that you can trick your brain into
thinking you are happy if you smile.
It also takes fewer muscles to grin
than it does to frown. How's that
for another simple way to wash away
the worries? The best things in life
are free, but you already know that.

You throw a feel-good party in
your brain every time you smile.

44

HAVE A NAP

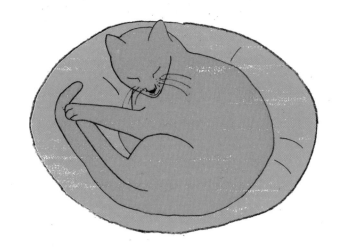

Taking a cat nap is different from getting more sleep. You can restore your equilibrium with a well-timed 30-minute siesta and get back to your work, family and friends feeling like a spring chicken. If you have trouble sleeping or wake up tired, a nap is the solution. Many people fall asleep while doing deep breathing exercises or meditating, which is perfectly fine. The whole point is to relax. Whether you fall asleep, or just calm your mind and body down, you will reap the benefits of taking the time to rest (for any length of time).

Worried about losing your memory? Napping will improve your powers of recall.

45

BRAINSTORM SOLUTIONS

As the saying goes, there is more than one
way to skin a cat. I don't know about you,
but I find that felines are best enjoyed furry.
When you have spun yourself into a tizzy over
whatever worry you may be wallowing in, take
some time to open your trusty notebook and
brainstorm a few solutions to your problem(s).
Some people believe you have immeasurable
potential (which would suggest you have
immeasurable options), so why not get creative
and start problem-solving? FYI: This is one of
the best recommendations in the book.

 Figure a way out/through
/over/under/around your
obstacle. You can do it.

46 GO TO THE DOCTOR / DENTIST

Hypochondriac or not, worrying about your health will always be a thorn in your side. If you haven't seen a healthcare professional in a while, take a deep breath, pick up the phone and make an appointment. If you need a recommendation, ask your friends or family members for a referral. And if you don't have health insurance, shell out and get some. Without a healthy body and mind, you have nothing. No amount of emotional, material or spiritual wealth will matter if you are worried about your short- or long-term longevity.

The waiting room is a great place to catch up on your reading.

47

FIND A MENTOR

Mentors will give you recognition and encouragement, and support you in achieving your goals. With increased self-esteem and confidence in your corner, there is no limit to what you can accomplish. Mentors provide perspective on your path and processes, and offer their experience and expertise in your shared field or industry. Someone who has gone before you can challenge you to take risks, yet provide solutions to problems you may not have even considered. There is no better (or faster) way to effectively succeed in any endeavour than by finding and employing the wisdom of a mentor.

Ask someone who has
been there before.

STOP BEING SO NICE

Do you try to please everyone? How is that working? If everyone seems to be on their own 'trip' that's because they are. As long as you worry about accommodating everyone and their wishes (which is noble, but ultimately unfulfilling) you may always feel unappreciated. Once you begin prioritising what is important to you, you will find you gain respect and leeway. As long as you are depleting your own self-worth (while attempting to satisfy everyone else's) you will be miserable. Time for a change.

If you worry about being too nice, don't go overboard and be mean. Just be firm.

49

PLAN A DATE NIGHT

We often blame our significant others for the anxiety, stress and worries in our lives. But date nights are a good opportunity to do the opposite. The point is to be yourself, let your hair down and have fun. If it's been a while, and you and your partner/spouse are more like roommates than lovers, it's time to plan a date night. How did you meet? How did you feel? Where were you? What did you like most about him/her? Time to rekindle the magic and mystery. Who knows what could happen...

Rekindle the romance, strengthen your relationship and ultimately worry less.

TAKE A BUBBLE BATH

Ernie from *Sesame Street* penned the lyrics 'Rubber ducky, you're the one. You make bath time lots of fun. Rubber ducky I'm awfully fond of you.' First of all, schedule your bubble bath, if you have to. And choose your bath-time company carefully. Go for scented candles or bath salts, your favourite music, a glass of wine or your favourite cocktail. Just get out before you turn into a raisin.

Wash your worries away.

51

MAKE A VISION BOARD

Shakti Gawain, the personal development guru, refers to Vision Boards as Treasure Maps, as if you are creating your own path to the rich rewards you desire. The process of arranging images, words, colours, patterns and symbols that reflect your innermost ideas, wishes and goals is therapeutic and creative. This is also a way to unearth unconscious desires; you will be amazed at what gets cut out and glued onto the canvas in front of you. Even if you do not consider yourself artistic (there are no rules) creating a Vision Board is fun!

Grab the scissors, some magazines, a poster board, a glue stick and go for it.

52 WATCH VIDEOS OF CUTE ANIMALS

There are countless videos online
(of varying quality) featuring
baby, teenage and adult animals
giving it their all, just so you
can feel warm and fuzzy inside.
From elephants playing the piano
to dancing hamsters, you can fill
your days blissfully immersed in the
antics of the animal kingdom caught
on tape. When nothing else
works to weed out the
worries in your life,
go to your favourite
search engine and
follow the breadcrumb
suggestions until your
face hurts because
you can't handle any
more animals getting
trapped in the
cute machine.

 Aww...

53

SNACK ON FRUIT

Fruit is packed with sugar and calories, but also bursting with some of the nutrient-rich vitamins, minerals and anti-oxidants your body needs to battle the battalions of worry storming the gates of your temple. The bottom line is: Snacking on fruit beats snacking on junk food any day of the week. If you are lucky enough to be able to pick your fruit from a tree or bush in your neighbourhood or backyard, even better. Just stay away from the poisoned apples left on your doorstep by a stranger who called while the dwarfs were at work.

Faith yields good fruit.
Worry yields stewed fruit.

54

LISTEN TO YOUR FAVOURITE MUSIC

Everything is made of light and sound. So, in some ways, music (sound) makes up half of all things. So if you ever wanted super powers, listen to your favourite music and instantly witch or warlock your worries away. At the very least, belting out your favourite rock anthem or inspirational gospel hymn will distract you long enough to see your problems in a new light, and at most, may actually help you make positive (overdue) changes in your life. Music is magic.

Need a mental health minute?
Listen to your favourite music.

55

VOLUNTEER

Much fret comes from self-involvement. When worry digs its teeth into your mind, it's time to stop pandering to the gnawing knot in your stomach and start serving others with your time, money and energy. All it takes to quiet the concerns in your life is to help others improve their lives. There are countless ways you can put your talents and resources to use for the betterment of your community or neighbourhood. What are you good at? Who do you like to spend time with? What can you share?

Make new friends, advance your career and get more hugs (see page 49).

56 GET A HEADSTART ON YOUR DAY

If EEEE! EEEE! EEEE! or RAAR! RAAR! RAAR! (or however your alarm clock sounds to you) doesn't phase you one bit, getting a headstart on your day by waking up at the crack of dawn can do wonders to ward off worry. If you have not seen the sunrise in years (or ever), getting up before the sun will amaze you when you see how much you can accomplish (not that accomplishment and achievement are the secret to happiness and worrying less). And by the time 3 o'clock rolls around, it will feel as if whatever happened at 10am took place yesterday.

<u>You know the early bird gets the worm, right?</u>

57

THINK OPPORTUNITIES NOT PROBLEMS

90% of things you worry about never happen. Does this not put your worries in perspective? Reflect on your life for a minute. How many bad things happened? Very few, right? You are still here and all is relatively well. Whenever you find yourself worrying yourself into a tornado-like tizzy, ask yourself: What is the silver lining surrounding this dark cloud? Take a minute and think about all the blessings in disguise your 'problem' may be hinting at.

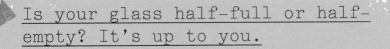

Is your glass half-full or half-empty? It's up to you.

58

COME OUT OF THE CLOSET (IF IT WOULD HELP)

You don't have to be gay to come out of any
room. But if you are, and the thought of
'exposing' your inner and outer true self
has you paralysed with fear and worry, it's
time to bare your soul to at least your best
friends (who probably have a hunch anyway).
And if you aren't gay, but hide in your
room or house or apartment and fear going
outside (how you got a hold of this book is a
mystery), hopefully you'll find the courage to
shine like the diamond you are. Whether the
world's a hostile or a friendly place is up
to you.

You are beautiful.

59

BE KIND TO YOURSELF

No one talks to you like you talk to yourself. Why do you berate and belittle your precious self? If you listen hard enough and reflect on your motivations, choices and worries, you may find the small voice of your 8-year-old self begging to be listened to, respected, played with and loved. But for some reason we all ignore, disrespect and exclude what we most deeply desire: a connection to what brings us joy.

Listen to the voice in your heart and respond with kindness.

GO TO THE GYM

If your clothes no longer fit and your waistline is worrying you, it's time to join a gym. Single? The gym is a great place to meet someone special (it's called a meat-market for a reason). Heck, if this turns out to be your scene, stick around until February (when 90% of new members renegotiate their self-improvement resolutions and choose the couch over the bench-press machine) and you will start to see results. Feeling lazy? You can drive there. Don't worry; everyone does.

 Personal trainers are cheaper than divorce attorneys.

DON'T READ THE NEWSPAPER

For some reason, conflict, suffering and controversy are attractive to people. Without this ammunition, the newspaper industry may not have ever existed to the extent it does. Yes, newspapers are full of good news, but the good is often overshadowed by the bad. So if you are sensitive to the drama of life and find yourself emotionally crippled by news of the worst, then stop reading the newspaper.

Fear, drama and disaster dominate the headlines.You don't need more to worry about.

62 THROW WORRY OFF THE SCENT

Worrying can cause health problems. In a hospital study, essential oils were diffused in the nurses' station, and researchers found the refreshing and revitalising aroma of grapefruit (one of the oils tested) reduced fatigue, stress and burnout. Heck, any essential oil with a pleasant smell that brightens your mood and makes you feel good will work. Bonus: Smelling a grapefruit can also aid weight loss. So wish worry a safe and happy holiday, and carry on making positive choices in your life.

Humans can detect one trillion distinct scents, so pick your favourite.

PLAY WITH YOUR KIDS

Angels and demons, kids are sent from both heaven and hell. But don't we all have a little bit of light and dark inside us? These little beings are simply closer (in time and space) to the place from wherever we all came from, and thus haven't been as tarnished by and assimilated into society as the rest of us. Playing with your kids will make you feel young again (you know this already). But if you don't have any kids of your own, go hang out with your nieces and nephews, or your friends' kids. Aside from looking at things from a new perspective, you might even learn something new about yourself.

Worried about aging? Summon your inner child and get dirty/silly/wild.

64

REWARD YOURSELF

What do you treasure? What makes you feel special? When was the last time you celebrated yourself just for being you? Put aside some time and/or money specifically for the purpose of pleasing yourself. Honouring 'you' is one of the finest forms of self-care. Without self-care, self-respect or self-confidence, worry is waiting around every corner, ready to pounce. And that's no way to live. Acknowledge yourself for the little things you do. Recognise your contribution(s) to the people and the world around you, and you will dispel (and finally put to bed) any nagging worries about your self-worth. For good.

Treat yourself to the best. You are worth it.

CREATE A BUDGET

Finances stress some people out more than anything else (and for good reason). Ever since the masses adopted currency as their means of exchange (instead of shells and livestock) most have suffered; but only because of an ignorance of basic economic principles like budgeting. Software and professionals abound to help you get your financial affairs in order. Keeping a simple notebook or spreadsheet of all the money you spend on petrol and groceries is a good start, so write down every penny you spend from now on, and review it every month.

Are you a master or a slave to money? Don't suffer; become the former.

LIMIT YOUR RESPONSIBILITIES

If you are a mature adult, you have responsibilities (how many has been up to you). If you are feeling overwhelmed, best not take on any more. The simpler your life, the fewer worries you will have. You won't be as distracted, entertained or persuaded, but if you can learn to live with fewer duties and tasks demanding your time, attention and resources, there is a good chance you will be happier (if less worry equals happiness, that is).

The wisest people in history have known the benefits of simplicity.

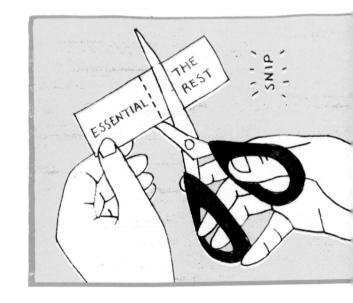

67 SING

Singing will distract you from your worries.
You can trick your brain into thinking you
are happy by singing or humming your
favourite tune. Doing this will also
help you breathe deeper (which,
as you know, can help to reduce
stress and worry). Exercising
your vocal chords is also
much cheaper than therapy,
healthier than drinking and
more fun than working out.
Do you know the lyrics to
your favourite song? Put it
on now and sing along.

Singing will cast
out the demons
of worry from
your life.

EAT A GOOD BREAKFAST

Allegedly, breakfast is the most important meal of the day. One way to look at your body is to view it like your car (which makes food your fuel). How does your car run on bad (or no) fuel? Research shows that if you miss breakfast, your body may not be able to handle the nutritional needs of the day (even if you pack them in later on), and you are more likely to reach for fatty, sugary snacks before lunch.

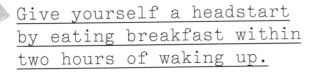

Give yourself a headstart by eating breakfast within two hours of waking up.

69

GET A MAKEOVER

Wardrobe. Check. Hair. Check. Accessories. Check. Shoes. Check. Makeup. Check. Overwhelming? You can find a fashionista at most retail stores who craves the challenge and opportunity to give a complete stranger a makeover. And they will do it for free. Set aside some loot (it doesn't have to be much) for your glamorous metamorphosis (it's no fun if you're worried about money) and enjoy the transformation. How often do you get to create a 'new' you? Do this as often as is necessary, though don't get carried away.

Who doesn't love a makeover?

70 SNAP A RUBBER BAND

A doctor interviewed by Woman's Day shared
a clever way to reduce worry. She suggests
keeping a rubber band around your wrist and
snapping yourself every time you start to
worry about something. This is a flexible way
to remind yourself to simply redirect your
thoughts to something positive. And if you are
one of those people who worry that you may
never be able to stop worrying, this might
just be the trick to literally snap you out
of it.

Be like rubber and let
worry bounce off of you.

GET THE FACTS

Before you fly-off-the-handle, get the facts. No point in worrying about what you can't control. Your reputation is out of your hands, so there's no need to get your knickers in a knot. Even when others are spreading rumours about you and your (mis) deeds, it's only because they are jealous. Brush it off and get on with your life (which is too short as it is).

Don't worry until you have all the information. There is most likely no need to fret.

QUIT WORRYING

72

TIDY YOUR DESK

How does the saying go? Disorganised desk, disorganised mind. And a disorganised mind breeds worry (not to mention stress, anxiety, health problems and even more disorganisation). Clutter is the enemy of freedom and fulfillment. If you have ever left home, you have most likely dragged an over-loaded suitcase or backpack far enough that you came close to disowning it (you are not alone). Travelling light at home, at work and at play, knowing you are 'on top of things', is a great way to worry less. Tidy your desk.

If you can find that receipt/
phone number/favourite coffee
cup, life will flow more easily.

73

BE SELFISH

Most of us were taught not to be selfish.
We were taught to be generous with
our resources and to share openly with
others. But you can't give someone a
ride if you don't have any petrol in
the tank. So, if something isn't a
resounding YES, then why not kindly
refuse to participate/purchase/commit?
Your personal time, money and energy are
precious resources to be cherished and
invested wisely.

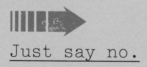

Just say no.

74

DO ONE THING AT A TIME

As much as you (and extremely productive people) may believe otherwise, experts say that humans are not wired for multitasking. Regardless of what you think, your brain can only focus on one thing at a time. For example, it will take you longer to complete two tasks when you are multitasking than if you were to do one thing at a time.

Multitasking
doesn't work.
Period.

75

HAVE FAITH

Doubt can be paralysing. Add a little worry to the mix, and you have a deadly cocktail. But don't fret, young grasshopper. Having faith that you will deal with whatever malady may befall you will help you overcome any obstacle, climb over any barricade, duck any flying object, squeeze through any crack and deke out any goaltender you ever encounter. Without faith, you have nothing. But with optimism, you avoid the suffering leading up to the issue you were worried about in the first place. Why not do whatever it takes to trust in your ability to do whatever it takes to get through any challenge you face?

Definition: Complete trust or confidence in someone or something.

Not sure how you're going to pay the rent or mortgage next month? Trust in your ability to earn enough to keep you from sleeping under a bridge. Sell your body to science if you have to.

Faith in the unknown is a risky business, but how do you think anyone gets anything done? Visionaries see things that others don't. Every manmade material object was once nothing but a thought. Every creator/inventor had faith in his/her creation.

Worried that everyone is out to get you? Being paranoid is no way to live. So why not have faith that people are generally friendly, helpful, considerate and kind? Either way, whatever you believe, you are right.

Religious people have faith in a higher power. How else do they know with so much certainty that everything exists on purpose? If you are a heathen (who isn't?) and worry yourself sick most of the time, maybe it's time to put your faith in the unknown, because ultimately, belief is the best guarantee.

Stressed out because you worry all the time? Put on your thinking cap and brainstorm a solution (or three) to your imminent problems. Remember: Becoming a creative problem-solver is a highly sought-after skill, both personally and professionally.

76

GIVE SOMETHING AWAY

Material possessions can be anchors, dragging along behind us when all we want to do is catch a gust of wind and sail toward a tropical island. You probably have a closet/basement/garage/attic/trunk/drawer filled with items you have not used in more than a year.

A good friend of mine — a student of happiness, time management and positive parenthood — lives by this philosophy: If he hasn't used something in the last year, he gives it away. This approach is not for everyone, though if you saw how much joy he shares with his family and friends (instead of worrying about/insuring/storing more stuff than he needs) you may just open that drawer or closet door and wonder:

What could I give away?

Is your stuff serving or suffocating you?

NIBBLE ON CHOCOLATE

Recent studies show that nibbling on dark (not milk) CHOCOLATE can calm your nerves. The Journal of Proteome Research fed their human guinea pigs 45g (1.5oz) of dark chocolate per day for two weeks and measured their stress hormones. Not surprisingly, the participants were not only less stressed, but also HAPPIER.

We do tend to spike and crash when riding the sugar rollercoaster, but when worry has you in its clammy clutches, what better way to cast out the demons of fear than by celebrating life with the uplifting (caffeinated) effects of rich, near-bitter dark chocolate?

A chunk of chocolate a day keeps the worries away.

78 PRETEND THE OPPOSITE IS TRUE

This simple, yet incredibly sophisticated mind game may just be the answer to gaining perspective on every problem.

Pretend you are worried that you won't get the job you just applied for. Instead of losing sleep over what may or may not happen, imagine you have been offered the job. Of course, if you don't get the job, then you will be disappointed. But until you know either way, there is no point in worrying about it.

Or if you are worried a loved one is up to no good, simply pretend they aren't. The fact that you are worried is proof that you don't have all the facts. If it turns out they are up to no good, then you can deal with it.

Do all you can to direct the nouns in your life in positive ways, and you will naturally negate any need to worry in the first place.

What if there wasn't anything to worry about?

LET GO OF YOUR PAST

Spiritual leaders since the beginning of time have hinted that while the future is a mystery, the past is history. Stop and consider that the only moment that exists in the time-space continuum is NOW. Whatever happened one second ago doesn't exist anymore (nor do you have any idea of what may happen five minutes from now).

These same spiritual teachers suggest that any fear or worry arises out of 'living' in the past by remembering — in vivid technicolour — all the negative experiences we dealt with (or didn't). Yes, knowing enough to not repeat our 'mistakes' is helpful, but dwelling on bygones will only keep us hobbling around on crutches, when all that is required to heal our hurts is to accept them as steps on the path and let them go.

Leave the past behind you.

FOCUS ON WHAT vs HOW

Some of the best motivational and spiritual teachers speak about focusing on the end result. Instead of getting bogged down in the details and challenges of 'how' you are going to achieve your goal, take one small baby step at a time, doing whatever is necessary in each moment. You will never be able to guess every outcome. And finally, the only reason you are worried is because you haven't committed to doing whatever it will take to accomplish your goal.

Follow the breadcrumbs and trust the process.

81

MOONLIGHT

There are 24 hours in a day, so if you are worried about making the car payments or buying bananas, you can always get a part-time job, or better yet, learn how to make a bit of money online. Expecting to get rich overnight can quickly leave you disappointed, so take it slow, do your research and enjoy the process. Who knows what you could create?

After the kids go to bed, don't watch Netflix, get to work.

82

STOP WONDERING WHAT OTHER PEOPLE ARE THINKING

We all do this. It's not our fault. It's human nature to compare ourselves to others. But the truth is, most people are too busy thinking about what your opinion of them is to spend time judging you and your wardrobe, home, friends, family or rusty old clunker.

What a relief! Fewer misconceptions cause greater stress in our lives. There are roughly seven billion ways to do everything (which would suggest you are free to do as you please), so why worry yourself sick about the irrelevant opinions of others any longer?

While you're worrying about what they're thinking, they're worrying about what you're thinking. Stop!

83 IMAGINE THE WORST CASE SCENARIO

<u>ASK YOURSELF:</u> What is the worst that could happen?

If more than one thing comes to mind, get out a pen and paper and write down as many imaginary tragedies that could possibly befall you. Pretend you are writing a horror movie script and imagine some far-out consequences to your wee little worries, because you know that most of what you worry about never comes true, right? Why not use your imagination to start dreaming up good things you want instead?

<u>Stop thinking about what you fear, and replace it with your goal.</u>

'If I get fired and can't find another job, the worst that could happen is my landlord (or bank) will kick me out of my apartment. I will have to go on welfare and live in a cardboard box under a bridge. On the upside, I will learn the art of entrepreneurship by squeegeeing car windshields at stop lights for spare change.'

'If my car gets stolen, the worst that could happen is I have to walk to a payphone, call a friend or cab for a ride, file a report with the police, call the towing companies and my insurance company. The upside? I get to shop for a new car.'

'If I lose touch with my friends, the worst that could happen is I may feel lonely for a while. On the upside, I get to start a new life and make new friends. Who knows who is out there waiting to party?'

'If I never meet a suitable marriage partner, I will have to fend for myself, and will eventually die alone. On the upside, dancing with exotic strangers on a singles cruise is more appealing than babysitting an antisocial spouse who was born with two left feet.'

'If my pet dies, the worst that could happen is I will miss him/her. On the upside, I will be reminded of the good times. Remembering how much joy we shared will ease the pain. And when the time is right, I will find another pet to love.'

84

WRITE YOUR WORRIES DOWN

You can always burn or shred the evidence if it's really painful or embarrassing, but for now, try not to judge your thoughts and feelings. If you hate or despise someone or something, say so. If you are scared of something, write about it. If you can't sleep or eat or think clearly, let your fingers do the walking and scribble/doodle until there is nothing left floating around in your brain.

Releasing your thoughts should start to get them out of your head and organising them on paper may help you begin to make sense of them.

Ignore your inner editor and let your problems spill onto the page.

DO SOME HOUSEWORK

Unless you are one of the rare humans who enjoys keeping everything spotlessly clean, housework lurks around every corner. However, some simple scrubbing can help distract you from your worries. And there are other perks — a tidy home gives you space to breathe, while a job well done brings a sense of accomplishment.

Hmmm. It appears that cleanliness is next to godliness.

Clear out your kitchen cupboards. Do you know what's lurking at the back of your kitchen cupboards? Face the unknown by getting everything out, throwing away anything that is past it's use-by date or not good for you and restore control and order.

Clean the oven. When did you last clean your oven? All that build-up of grease and grime is not good for you. So confront it head on and tackle it with all you've got — sprays, scrubbers and elbow grease.

Vacuum under and behind furniture. Instead of doing a quick once-over, pull all the furniture out and vacuum behind and underneath it. The workout will be good for body, mind and spirit.

Ironing. Smooth away creases, crinkles and cares and watch the pile of clean clothes and tasks achieved build up beside you.

Make your bed with fresh sheets. Is there anything nicer than getting into a newly made bed? Picture a fresh start and have a good night's sleep — one of life's best medicines.

86

CREATE AN EMERGENCY PREPAREDNESS KIT

No one can tell the future. Which is why being prepared for the worst is a wise decision. At the very least, keep some blankets, candles, matches, water, flares and a wind-up radio in the trunk of your car, because you never know what can happen. Better to be safe than sorry, right? Some folks think it prudent to build bomb shelters, so if it will ease your anxiety, take emergency preparedness as far as you like (regardless of what the neighbours think).

Being prepared will help you worry less if/ when things happen.

87 MAKE A DECISION

Successful people make decisions fast and change slowly, whereas unsuccessful people make decisions slowly, though change their minds fast. Which one are you? Who do you want to be? When you make a decision (big or small), you have made up your mind, and thus you can stop worrying. There are pros and cons to everything, no matter what you decide. You are on earth to learn and grow. When you were learning to walk, how many times did you fall down? It didn't matter. You got up and kept on going. The only wrong decision you will ever make is to continue worrying about making the wrong decision.

No decision is equivalent to no movement.

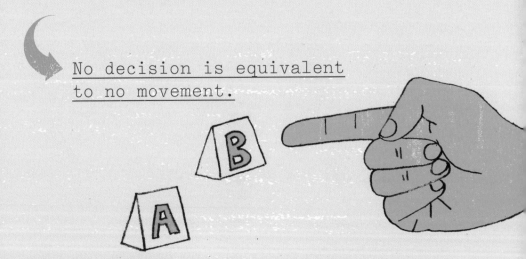

88

SHARE YOUR FEELINGS

If you are worried you may be misunderstood or not heard, you must speak up. As long as you keep your worries bottled up, no one can ever help. Does someone need to know how you feel? The sooner you share your fears and worries with the people you care about, perhaps the less these goblins will haunt you. Wouldn't that be nice? No one was born an expert communicator, but sharing your feelings is a skill that can be learned. Begin by asking someone you trust to listen.

If true communication is hearing what isn't said, what is your body language saying?

89

REGISTER FOR A COURSE

Personal and professional development is a billion-pound industry for a reason (as is traditional post-secondary education). Even continuing education or online courses offered via your local college can give you the necessary skills to change careers or get a raise or promotion. However, if you can't travel or don't have the time, complete a correspondence course at your own pace (which you may find faster than if you attend a weekly in-class session or lecture).

The more you learn, the more you earn.

 # 90 TAKE SOMEONE OUT FOR LUNCH

After breakfast, lunch is the second most important meal of the day. And what better way to enjoy midday than with someone you like, love or admire? Lunch can be simple and quick, or it can be complex and last the afternoon. It's up to you and your company. Grab a smoothie and go  for a walk around the block, or get a bottle of wine, share a collection of appetisers and relax. Better yet, go for lunch once a week with someone state-of-the-art. Make it a tradition. The more you connect with other people, the less you will worry (and the more you will learn).

 Suggest eating dessert first.

GET SUPPORT

If worry has you on the brink of dread, get some support. No matter what form of support you choose (or finds you) everyone needs help at some point. Which is why numerous support groups exist to ease every human fear and fault (real or imagined). Some cost money and some are free, but what else is money for? Without a healthy mind, body and spirit, no purchase will alleviate the concerns that plague you. Sometimes, the only way 'out' is 'through', so why not confront the voices that keep you afraid and deal with whatever issues are nagging at you?

You are not alone.

92 QUIT YOUR JOB IF YOU HAVE TO

The average worker stays at their job for 4.6 years, so quitting a job is not uncommon. If you dread going to work, is there any way you could (responsibly) quit? Is there any way you can reduce your expenses or increase your income? Can you rent a room in your house? If you can live on less, you don't need to work as much to cover your monthly expenses. Yes, being temporarily uncomfortable may be uncomfortable, but how much do you value your sanity? If your job is a major source of worry, you must do something positive and productive to remedy the situation. Just tread lightly.

If you want to be in show business, get out of the factory!

93

TAKE SOME VITAMINS

Thanks to factory farming, and processed/ packaged foods, supplementing your diet with vitamins and minerals is a wise way to ward off the worries when it comes to your health and well-being. Even if you shop at your local farmers' market and eat primarily organic food, you may still be missing out on some vital nutrients from your food. But your body has different needs at different stages in your life, so it's best to consult a nutritionist, naturopath or physician to get proper recommendations for the supplements most suited to you, your body and your lifestyle.

'Take your vitamins.' ~ Hulk Hogan, World Wrestling Federation Champion.

BE ON TIME

Take the edge off every appointment, plan and commitment you have by being on time. Show your friends, family, colleagues, clients and coworkers that you hold them in high regard. If you know you are often late, plan to leave earlier. Running late is stressful, so go easy on yourself and your schedule. There are enough hours in each day to be on time. By doing so, you will maintain a sense of balance that will help you manage everyone and every responsibility in your busy schedule.

Show respect for other people, and other people will show respect for you.

95

HONE YOUR SKILLS

Whatever you do, you can do better. Not wishing to sound like an over-achieving parent or boss, but the more you hone your skills, the more attractive you become to friends, family, colleagues and your chosen industry. If you are worried about becoming obsolete, irrelevant or replaceable (at home or work) simply develop, improve and broaden your skill set. Invest time, money and energy in bettering your life.

Get better at something and you will worry less about living a meaningful/less life.

96

START A SAVINGS ACCOUNT

If you started saving 10% of your babysitting, lawn mowing and lemonade stand money, you developed a practical habit. But even if you didn't, it's not too late to start saving for a rainy day. The more money you have in the bank, the less you will worry. Still, so many people live pay cheque-to-pay cheque (probably because they never learned the benefits of saving and investing their hard-earned loot). Worrying about money will stress you out more than most things, so if you want to put your mind at ease, start saving 10% of everything you earn.

➤ It rains.

97

EXPRESS YOURSELF CREATIVELY

Do you have a vivid imagination? Do you feel the urge to make something out of nothing? Do you see things others don't? Are you fascinated by colour, texture, form, sound or images? If you answered yes to any of these questions (and you haven't yet experimented with wood, clay, cloth, metal, ink, glass, pixels, paper, sound or any organic material capable of being moulded and transformed into something else entirely), would you agree it's time to start playing with your food?

Interpret what you feel/think / see/hear/taste in a new way, and you will be amazed.

Save £100. Book a date with yourself for the afternoon. Go to the art-supply shop. Ask the sales assistant about the characteristics of different materials and tools, and what results you can expect. Take some art supplies home with you and use them.

While listening to music, ask yourself what instrument best defines you. Find a music teacher and sign up for lessons. Practise regularly. The more you play, the better you will get. And the better you get, the more you will play.

Find a reputable course to teach you how to write code. Learning how to create software from nothing but a keyboard gives you unlimited creative (and earning) potential.

Join a pottery, blacksmithing, glass-blowing, knitting, paper-sculpture or cooking class — in fact, numerous courses exist for you to learn about different forms of artistic self-expression. So what are you waiting for?

Write the book you have simmering inside you. With the advent of self-publishing, and with a well-researched idea, you can make your mark on the world. Cookbook, memoir, self-help manifesto or novel, taking the risk to write and/or publish a book will erase worry like few other creative endeavours.

98

STOP BLAMING OTHER PEOPLE

Blaming other people for your problems is immature. As much (and as often as) other people seem to be the cause of all your worries, concerns and problems, they are not (and never will be). Eleanor Roosevelt said that no one can make you feel anything without your permission. Until you take 100% responsibility for your life, you will likely continue to worry (and thus never be happy with anyone or anything good that comes your way).

→

Victims will never be happy. If you want to be happy, remember: you are your choices.

99

HAVE AN ORGASM

Why do we do anything? Because we are motivated to feel good. Basically, sexual ecstasy is responsible for perpetuating our entire species. If orgasms didn't feel so good, relieve so much stress and bring us so much satisfaction, humanity wouldn't exist. So praise sunshine, water and sex for everything and everyone. It really is this simple, so if after reading every other page in this book you are still worried about something, you know what to do.

Woohoo!

100

DO NOTHING

If a genie ever granted you three wishes,
and you spent two tokens on emotional and
material success, chances are — like most
people — you would opt for world peace.
And, like most people, you also consider
yourself 'good'. That means Edmund Burke
hit the nail on the head when he said,
'The only thing necessary for the triumph
of evil is for good people to do nothing.'
But the simplest concepts are often the
hardest to grasp, which is why you must
consider what he meant, for the sooner our
collective wish comes true, the sooner
books like this will be history.

By doing nothing, you do
nothing wrong. And have
nothing to worry about.

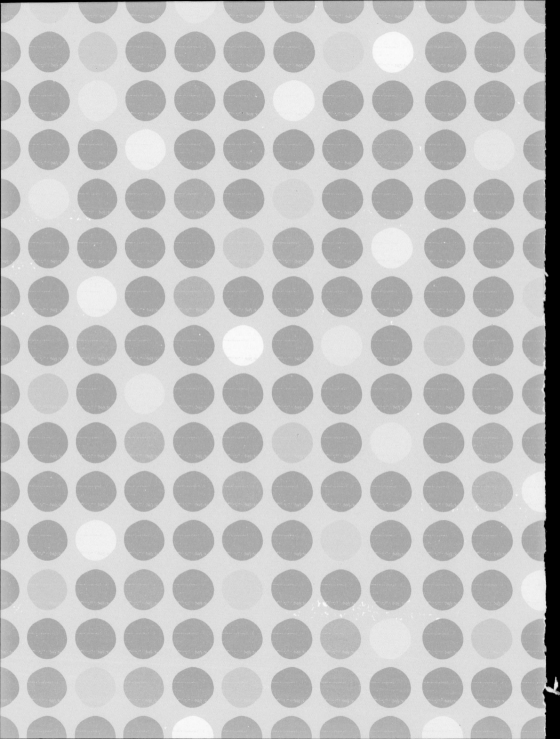